Rogers Marvel Architects

Rogers Marvel Architects

Rob Rogers and Jonathan Marvel

Princeton Architectural Press · New York

Our practice thrives on diversity. For almost twenty years we have collaborated and cajoled our way from a small, two-person firm that started much like many other architecture practices to the multidisciplinary practice we are today. We did what we could to get by and at the same time focused our interests toward a long-term trajectory. Throughout this period, we never set predetermined boundaries for our explorations and work.

We couple our commitment to build with an intrigue for design at all scales with a belief in the necessity of beautiful things. Early work for residences and small renovations has taken us to buildings and parks, to architecture for all things—in, around, and beyond the city. As Charles Eames wrote, "Everything is architecture."

Our work comes from a passionate and collaborative studio practice. We engage in debate, inviting ideas and voices from within and without. The process is dynamic, intense, and fun. The yield is a growing portfolio, a portion of which is included here, that lets us pursue inhabitation from almost every perspective. By initially focusing on museums and galleries and working with artists, we found an affinity for discovery and developed an appreciation for the unexpected.

At the heart of our architectural practice is communication. The discussion between the architect and client is the beginning of our creative process. Asking the right questions, for example, can enable new solutions. Having a partner builds the collaborative effort into the fundamental nature of the practice. This permeates through the rest of the design professionals in the studio, resulting in a horizontal sharing of experience, intuition, and inventiveness in a studio without walls. We rely on this continuous dialogue to discover the unknown destination.

We make physical models of everything because we feel it is still the best tool in the design world. The model, in all its multiple iterations, from sketch to final rendition, allows decisions to be made efficiently and in a progressive way. A repetition of forms with gradual adjustment creates a sense of confidence in unexplored territory.

Relying on a wide array of studies in an unfinished state has given our projects a thread of continuity despite their distinct differences. Projects evolve from problem solving and program into an exploration of material and organization. From this we have derived six guidelines (if not full-fledged principles) that help us develop an understanding of design that can inform a new sanctuary, a rural park, or a subway grate. These are few and simple: 1. the role of light must be crafted with precision, 2. materials are best used with authenticity, 3. the distinction between architecture and sculpture is program, 4. every surface deserves equal attention, 5. clear concepts underlie beautiful solutions, and 6. paint is not a material.

Our inspirations come from every part of our lives: from a fascination for the work of our peers, to an intimately crafted Finnish fishing float, to the ambitions of Buckminster Fuller who asked, "What does humanity need and how can I find a solution?" To build is to study and learn.

Rob Rogers and Jonathan Marvel

Introduction
Michael Sorkin

At some time in my adolescence, for reasons not entirely clear
to me, I developed a powerful jones for all things Swedish. As a bien-
pensant preteen socialist, I was totally into the welfare state, not to
mention Anita Ekberg, and as a tyke, having been given a copy of
The City in History by my mother, I was persuaded that Vällingby,
with its delightful street lamps and square-windowed towers, was the
omega point of urban civilization. I suspect that I knew more about
Sven Markelius than any boy in Fairfax County, Virginia.

One of the comforting, corroborating aspects of Swedish
modern architecture was the pitched roofs on otherwise
contemporary-looking buildings, an obvious violation of the
canon. This was particularly important to me since we lived in such
a modernist house, with a pitched roof, in a neighborhood—designed
by a single architect—that included similar houses with either flat
or so-called "butterfly" roofs. Worried at the wanting purity of my
environment, I took great comfort in the fact that the Swedes—
the most modern people of all—thought nothing of such a seeming
contradiction. Indeed they produced a succinct and completely
functionalist argument for it: it snows! It snowed on our house too!

I keep thinking about that pitched roof, not so much because
it exceeds some important boundary of taste, but because it suggests
the elasticity of a rational approach to modernist architecture.
If any issue confronts our architecture with special clarity nowadays,
it's the question of environment, and that pitched roof suggests the
kind of self-evident inflection all our buildings must engage. Funny
about that house of ours, though. The roof was pitched, but the walls
of glass and the tiny operable windows positioned low down led
to a nightmare of solar gain. The architect was clearly conflicted,
unable to push the last measure of practicality against the resistance
of his design religion.

Rob Rogers and Jonathan Marvel are architects of flexibility
and verve and of a kind of Scandinavian neighborliness. Operating
from a default of simplicity—a quality quite different from minimal-
ism with its fetish for the reductive—they have produced a body
of work that beautifully balances social and formal richness and
reserve. Their houses, replete with pitches and a fine, easy, sense of

the environment (a commitment also clearly reflected in their extensive pursuit of adaptive reuse), are at once rigorous and casual, laid-back and self-confident. They unfold from their own livability rather than founding habitation simply on the empty constrictions of taste. The larger buildings are cannily organized, rhythmically subtle, and materially refined (I find repeated delving into the Stephen Gaynor School on the Upper West Side of Manhattan especially rewarding). They are also just right in the way they provide unexpected and exceptional events and tectonic surprises. At Gaynor, they split the main structure into splayed columns that sit on big transfer beams, a move that's at once practical and animating. The same spirit lies behind the beautiful flying room at the Whaler's Lane Residence, which captures a view and lets the composition take off.

For me, though, what really distinguishes Rogers Marvel Architects is not simply the lovely sense of craft and detail, the measured modernity of the architectural expression, or even the more formally adventurous projects—like the Nativity Church project in La Primavera, Mexico, or the Jeff-Koons-meets-Kermit-the-Frog restrooms at Mill River Park in Connecticut. Despite their mastery of and comfort with forms that resist the flashiness of arbitrary avant-gardism, RMA are authentic pioneers in the elision of architecture, landscape, and infrastructure, in a very careful consideration of the ideas behind the possibility of contemporary public space, in the creation of a unified project of terrestrial form-making. They do stay in touch with their Scandinavian side.

Here, too, they recover something of Vällingby's charms. That place is etched in memory largely because of those tree-like street lamps that seemed to animate the plaza at the project's core. As a kid, I was especially fascinated by the expanded field of what would now be called street furniture, including light standards, gas pumps, highway guardrails, columns supporting the bridges over the interstate, and other features of the industrial landscape. RMA seem to like this stuff too and show an elegant mastery over a series of urban appliances, including their striking—and totally sui generis—flood-prevention gratings for the New York City subway and their magical proposals for a landscaped noise-abatement system at Amsterdam's Schiphol airport. Indeed, since I've known them (we had offices in the same building for years), what is most striking about the development of their practice is the truly suave growth of the landscape work, which, through a series of informative collaborations, is extremely graceful in aligning a tectonic imagination with a more literally and figuratively wild one.

This dialogue of free growth and constraint that informs the morphology of such projects as the Governors Island competition or Cody Park recurs philosophically in their renovation of the McCarren Pool, one of the monuments of the days of the "good" Robert Moses who for a time commanded a lovely—and very Swedish—approach to public architecture and infrastructure. But infrastructure is something that both does and doesn't have a fixed repertoire of roles, structures, and activities. The public park, pool, and beach are creations of modernity and mark the expansion of citizens' rights to exercise their freedom of collective leisure and sociability. They are emblems of our public selves, of what we share.

But of course there's a dark side. The critique of these places has always converged on society's motive to control, on the idea that modernism homogenizes publics that should be respected for their differences, that these places can be paradigms of exclusion, per the racism of Moses and his various strategies to deny African-Americans access to his designs, or the classism of the civilizing mission espoused by Frederick Law Olmsted for his parks. But it's wrong to dismiss these great places out of motives that are now lost to meaning, or because they are themselves conventional and do not necessarily represent the complete, always changing range of spaces that our multiple and shifting publics desire. RMA are completely plugged into these contradictions and have probably attracted the most attention as thoughtful striders of the line between the coercive possibilities of public space and the productive and expansive.

This has everything to do with 9/11. The building we shared was not far from Ground Zero, and much of the work in this volume is post-9/11 and indeed because of 9/11. RMA have become perhaps the best architects in America at the task of both reimagining urban landscapes with consideration for the threat of terror and at inventing the infrastructures and objects that secure them. The success of this effort is reflected in the style by and with which they are able to reappropriate or "deputize" familiar apparatuses like bollards, curbs, paving, planting, and sheltering for the purposes of civil defense in a way that is original (many of the objects and configurations are beautiful) and produces a mitigating dual use. This takes place both at the scale of object—their incredibly sturdy bollard-cum-seating objects are justifiably renowned—and at the scale of the system. To the degree that the lock-down of lower Manhattan has created a genuinely more pedestrian-friendly environment, the kinds of infrastructures designed by RMA for Wall Street or Battery Park City are highly positive developments for the cityscape.

I must admit, however, to a certain conceptual ambivalence about this type of work. There's a fine line between precaution and paranoia and my most reflexive reaction is to be nervous: I don't like to see the city fortified and I am certainly not confident that the exponential increase in surveillance is completely friendly to my interests. My qualms, however, are eased by RMA's approach. Whatever one may think about the motives of those who are instigating our newly anxious and militarized architecture (which has, to be sure, been part of the standard professional repertoire since Vitruvius first codified the scope of the discipline), the work that RMA has done in New York City is clearly a net gain for the city. The field of objects within the space of streets, parks, and extensions, has been made more elegant, traffic has been reduced dramatically, and attention has been devoted to a range of quotidian objects—from benches to barricades—that have too long been outside the field of our best designers.

Make no mistake here. Rogers and Marvel are among our best designers. Not simply for the lovely buildings, parks, and things they create but more importantly for their pioneering transcendence of a disciplinary isolation that increasingly seems like a relic. Their practice is full of consideration for the ways in which things and people sit together in nature and space. Their way of working and the projects they make are models for the future.

Buildings

Westchester Reform Temple
Scarsdale, New York

We always design for long-term use, efficiency, and beauty and we like
to think that practices now considered green have long been part
of our work. Westchester Reform Temple is our first project for a religious
institution and our first LEED-certified project. It embodies many of our
sustainable philosophies and sets a standard for spiritual space. The project
includes seventeen thousand square feet of sanctuary, social hall, lobby,
and kitchen spaces in a new building.

Upon entering the sanctuary, a visitor first notices the glowing east
sculptural glass wall. Fabricated with sophisticated bending and coating
technologies, this feature is both architecture and artwork—it reflects
the changing seasons in the adjacent garden, reduces solar gain, and
lights the sanctuary by day. At the same time, the wall reflects back the
congregation gathered together in the space.

The interlocking wood and plaster bands that define the sanctuary
space are an expression of *tikkun olam* or "repairing the world"—a belief
that the Jewish people must continually seek to mend an imperfect world.
The bands, alternating between traditional plaster construction and
cedar assemblies, never quite meet; they are held apart by an interstitial
skylight, struggling to reconcile. Tikkun olam requires constant and
repetitive effort, and this inherent conflict is made present in the basic
form and structure of the sanctuary.

Interpreting *tikkun olam*: interlocking
fingers held apart, not quite meeting,
separated by light

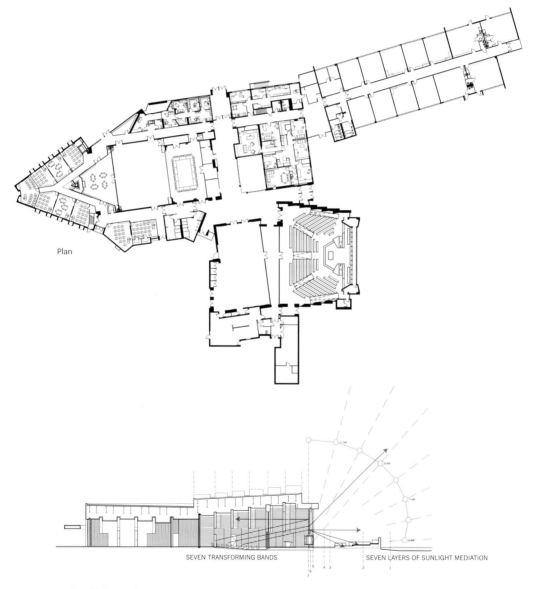

Plan

SEVEN TRANSFORMING BANDS   SEVEN LAYERS OF SUNLIGHT MEDIATION

Studies of light over the course of a day and year helped define the glass profiles for the east wall.

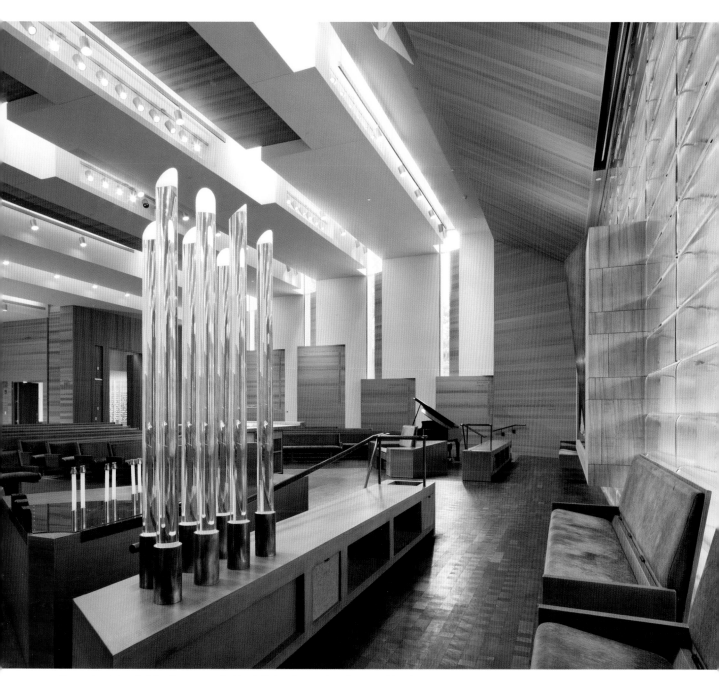

The sanctuary's form is defined by seven vertical bands that mark seven days of prayer and learning.
The final band at the east represents the Sabbath; it holds the Ark and frames the bimah.

State Street 14 Townhouses
Brooklyn, New York

Positioned between Brooklyn's downtown commercial core and its adjacent historic residential neighborhoods, 14 Townhouses is the first phase of a two-acre urban renewal project on a site vacant for seventy years. Many of the historic buildings were removed to allow construction of eight subway tracks beneath this city block. The south side of State Street is lined with an uninterrupted row of townhouses—all of them listed on the National Register of Historic Places.

14 Townhouses anchors the redevelopment by reconnecting the site to its historic residential neighbors. Each house is a modern interpretation of the classic townhouse type with stoops to re-create street life. Together, these houses establish a unified but lively street front; the composition of each house is subtly varied to create quiet but distinct differences that distinguish each house from its neighbors. A respectful dialogue between old and new guided our approach.

Taking design cues from the adjoining historic houses and those across the street, the townhouses' facade planes, assembly details, openings, and entries produce a visually compelling procession. Windows recessed eight inches make up for the lack of ornament. Stucco coloration produces subtle color variations in rear facades that face gardens that are extensions of the interior space, not separate from it.

Though each home is less than eighteen feet wide, the open floor plan, dramatic double-height wall of glass, sky-lit open stair, and oversized windows create a spacious and light-filled urban home. Development of fourteen individual homes provided us with a singular design opportunity: not since the late 1920s has New York City seen a new, uninterrupted block of market-rate townhouses.

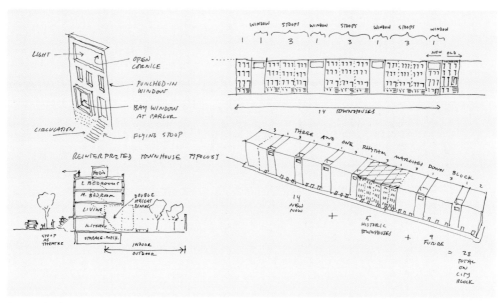

Concept sketches

Phase one, 14 Townhouses, opened in 2006. Phase two, 9 Townhouses, will take cues from the first fourteen, but have their own identity. Projected completion 2013.

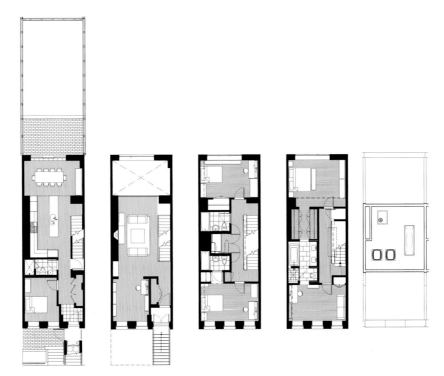

Plans for the units with stoop

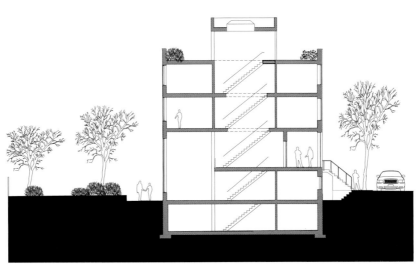

Section

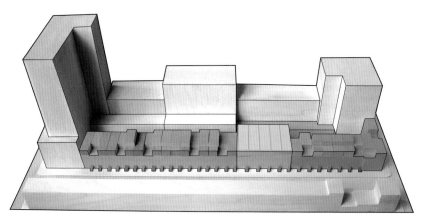

Site model showing the completed block

14 Townhouses (phase one) at left, five historic townhouses, and 9 Townhouses (phase two) at right will complete the block.

The Stephen Gaynor School
New York, New York

Could a new urban school tower embody the soul of the townhouse it would replace? This was our challenge when we won the invited competition for a new ten-story building for the Stephen Gaynor School. The school, established in 1963, had outgrown its brownstone on West 89th Street and the board wanted to build a new school that could better sustain their mission of nurturing young children with learning differences. We needed to keep several things in mind; for instance, the intimate feel of the brownstone was comforting to many of the students, particularly those with navigational and sensory difficulties. The school also wanted to keep class sizes small, offer individualized teaching within the classroom, and make kids feel secure in a much larger setting.

We developed a concept for two smaller, four-story schools, upper and lower, linked in the middle by a floor with shared art, science, occupational therapy, and music spaces. Classrooms have break-out spaces where therapists and teachers can work with students one-on-one, and where students can take movement breaks and employ other self-regulating techniques while remaining with the group.

Each school has its own stair; they meet in the middle of a continuous seven-story atrium. We designed the lower school stair with an internal focus, while the upper school stair reaches out toward the building perimeter, terminating at a window that looks out to the city and the larger community, of which the older children will soon become a part. The Gaynor School is the only educational facility in New York City with an interconnecting seven-story stair; there are no interruptions or fire enclosures. We sought approval from the Department of Buildings for this typically prohibited configuration by successfully arguing that a visually and spatially open stair was critical to the students' wayfinding and sense of place.

In conjunction with the fabricator, we developed a panelized facade system that could accept clay tile and copper, permitting most of the exterior to be constructed off-site and installed quickly within an extremely limited staging area.

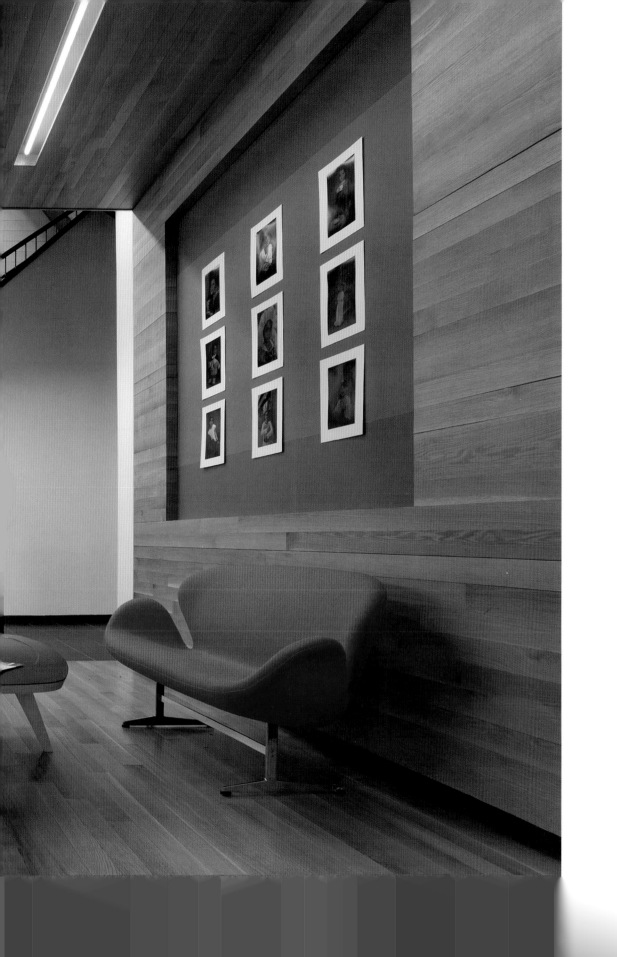

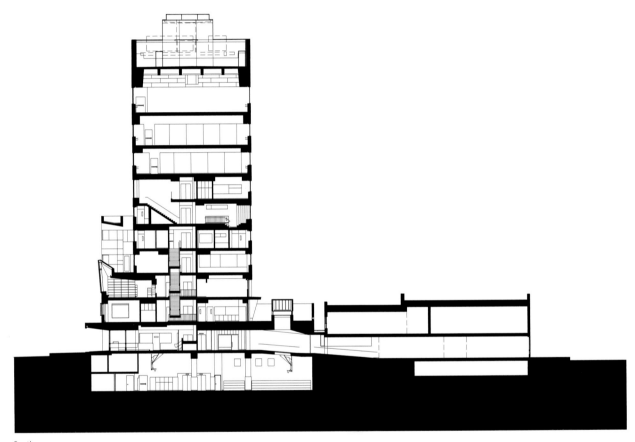

Section

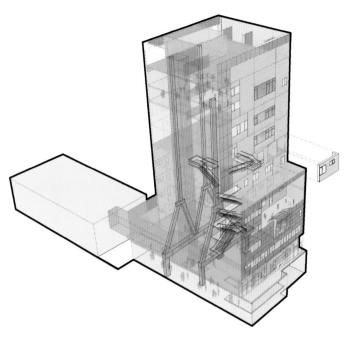

Composite diagram of the building's systems, structure, and program

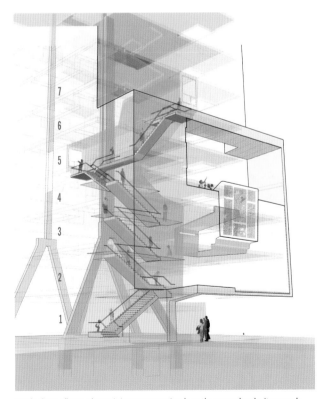

On the lower floors, the stair is more contained; on the upper levels, it expands toward the building perimeter, with views to the city from landings.

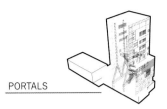

PORTALS

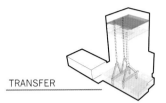

TRANSFER

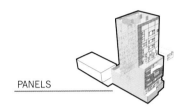

PANELS

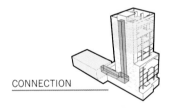

CONNECTION

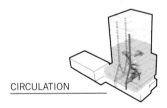

CIRCULATION

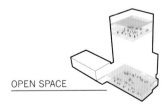

OPEN SPACE

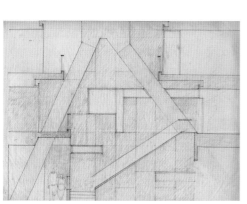

Interior sketch with concrete structure

North Fork Residence
Cody, Wyoming

Building in the Wyoming landscape means balancing a desire for views and openness with the realities of a climate that can be harsh and unforgiving. The North Fork residence, on the Shoshone River just outside Cody, does just that, protecting against heavy snow and drying sun and providing spaces for outdoor activity even in adverse conditions.

Our client, a New York antique furniture and lighting dealer, owned the site for thirty years before hiring us to design his house. In his bachelor days, he worked hunting season as a dude ranch wrangler, a respite from city life. His first dwelling on the site was a trailer, which grew ad hoc extensions to keep up with marriage and a growing family. Our work began as a renovation master plan, to make sense of the accumulation, and ultimately became a project for a new house.

We reclaimed cedar siding from earlier generations of dwellings on the site to build concrete formwork. The resulting deeply veined and weathered finish links the house to time and its own history. The concrete north porch extends into the house and becomes a massive hearth at its center. Several large boulders extracted nearby help form the fireplace. In this way, the landscape continues right through the house, from the north to the south. A series of outdoor rooms allow for year-round use. Some block the wind, some screen from rain, and others allow dappled sunlight to warm a terrace. Even when completely sheltered from the ever-present wind, you experience extraordinary long-range views out into the hills.
One of the owner's favorite features is a cocktail porch off the living room with unobstructed views of the distant mountains.

Reclaimed wood from the site was used to make the concrete formwork.

Site model

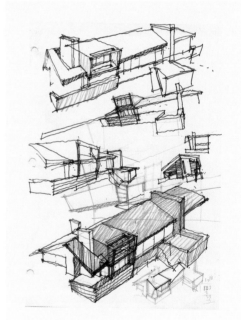

Early sketches

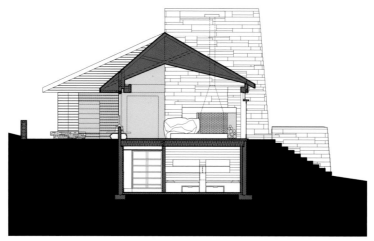

Section through the main living space, with monumental fireplace beyond

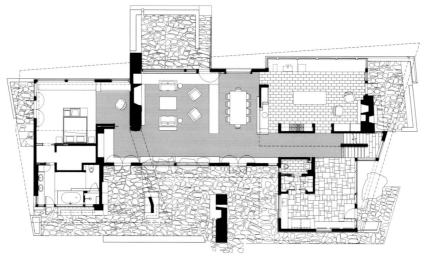

Floor plan. The large public living and kitchen space is flanked by outdoor rooms.
The small private zone is at the west end.

Whaler's Lane Residence
Amagansett, New York

The Whaler's Lane Residence began with a single cedar beach bungalow in Amagansett, New York. The property is located on the Atlantic coast, in a quiet neighborhood of eclectic beach homes. Although the site's original bungalow was weathered, lying within a tall field of beach grasses on the private side of an eroding dune, the attraction to this place was clear, as was the desire to preserve the tranquil nature and modesty of the residence.

With those goals in mind, the bungalow was renovated with the addition of a kitchen, guest rooms, guest studio, and outdoor pool. The now-protected dune that runs between the house and the oceanfront is the defining feature of the site. It creates a wall that separates the house's public town side from its private residence side, in addition to shielding it from strong winds. The view from the extended bedroom is made level with the dune's crest, obscuring the public beach and overlooking only the open ocean.

Great care was used to create modern warmth throughout the home. The finishes were selected from local materials and assembled by a team of local craftsmen who stayed on the project through its completion. As it stands now, the home represents a series of renovations all grown from the original beach vernacular. The additions have become a collection of shingle-wrapped exterior and interior spaces connected by wooden pathways. The deck space weaves in and out of the house. The shingles are made of lead-coated copper, while scrap slate from the step industry is cut into brick-like units and forms the house's chimneys.

The property is united by a strong desire to maintain the original character of the landscape, as well as the home, native grasses, and vegetation. Guests use long wooden beach palettes to protect the native landscape while walking from the house to the guest studio, and boardwalks to traverse the dune to a private seating area and the beach. The oversized shingle detail and wrap-under roof were inspired by Greene & Greene's Gamble House (1908) in Pasadena, California.

The cantilevered master bedroom reaches up over the dune to the maximum
zoning height in order to catch an ocean view.

Eyebeam Art + Technology Center
New York, New York
with Arup

Competitions are often the catalyst for new directions in an office, and
the Eyebeam competition inspired us to set our sights on larger-scale work.
Our entry in this invited competition for a new ninety thousand-square-
foot museum of art and technology in Chelsea's Arts district was one of
four finalists.

In addition to traditional exhibition and education missions, the Eyebeam
Museum was to include spaces for art production. To understand this
program, we organized a series of weekly seminars where digital DJs, new
media artists, and curators of technology-based art shared their thoughts
on modes of production, education, and exhibition of contemporary art.

Eyebeam Atelier would initially occupy only part of the structure, growing
into the space over time. The heart of the design became the circulation
spine. We developed ideas for moving through the project through a
series of mapping exercises that explored multiple routes to a common
destination—for example, from many homes to a common office. Ultimately,
we seized upon a ski map as the conceptual basis for our circulation
system, a rich model that embodies multiple means of ascent and descent,
flexible routes, and skill-based choices. A visitor to the museum chooses
a path based on their physical or intellectual capacity on any certain day.
The routes include opportunities for overlap and combined course,
frequently crossing into the areas of education and production. Visitors
can also move through the building as a more traditional exhibition
participant moving through exhibition spaces, as a student going through
a series of educational opportunities, or as a journalist or purchasing
agent moving through artist production areas.

Computer behaviors became metaphors for the architecture. Interleaving,
a process for constantly reorganizing varying amounts and types of
stored digital information, inspired a circulation strategy that could shift
over time. Overwriting, a process of saving new information on top
of old, informed our strategy for programmatic expansion, contraction,
and intensification.

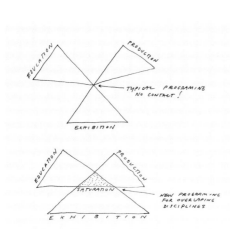

Concept sketch

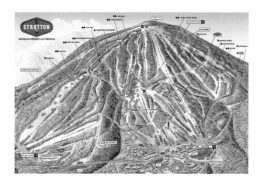

A ski map provided early inspiration for the scheme:
multiple paths to a common destination with a varied, skill-
based descent.

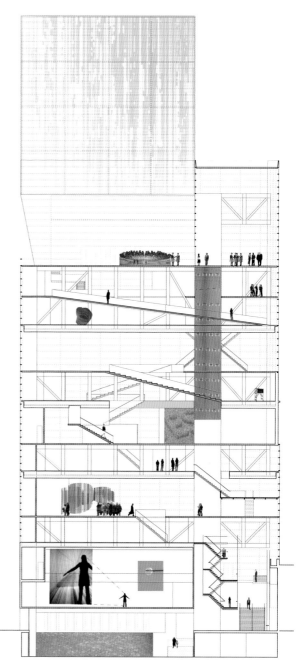

Section image

interleaved circulation

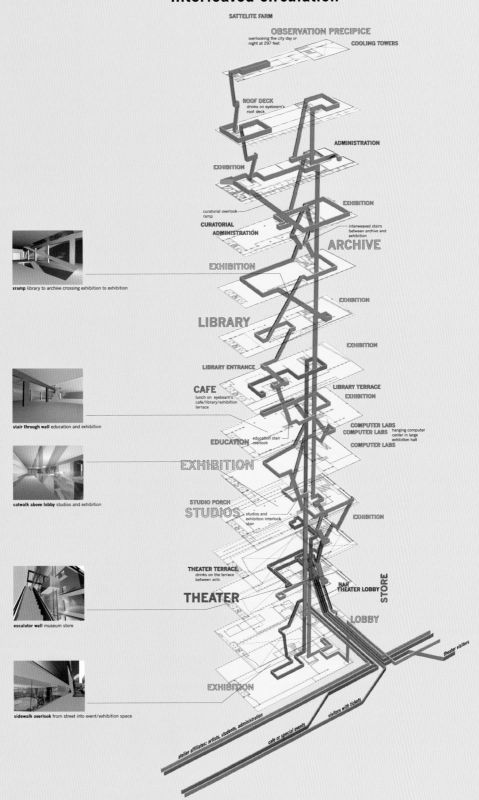

SATTELITE FARM

OBSERVATION PRECIPICE
overlooking the city day or
night at 297 feet

COOLING TOWERS

ROOF DECK
drinks on eyebeam's
roof deck

ADMINISTRATION

EXHIBITION

EXHIBITION

curatorial overlook
ramp

interweaved stairs
between archive and
exhibition

CURATORIAL
ADMINISTRATION

ARCHIVE

EXHIBITION

EXHIBITION

xramp library to archive crossing exhibition to exhibition

LIBRARY

EXHIBITION

LIBRARY ENTRANCE

LIBRARY TERRACE

CAFE
lunch on eyebeam's
cafe/library/exhibition
terrace

EXHIBITION

COMPUTER LABS
COMPUTER LABS

hanging computer
center in large
exhibition hall

stair through wall education and exhibition

EDUCATION

education stair
overlook

COMPUTER LABS

EXHIBITION

catwalk above lobby studios and exhibition

STUDIO PORCH

STUDIOS

studios and
exhibition interlock
stair

EXHIBITION

THEATER TERRACE
drinks on the terrace
between acts

BAR
THEATER LOBBY

STORE

THEATER

escalator wall museum store

LOBBY

EXHIBITION

sidewalk overlook from street into event/exhibition space

theater visitors

atelier affiliates: artists, students, administration

cafe or special events

visitors with tickets

Multiple overlapping routes

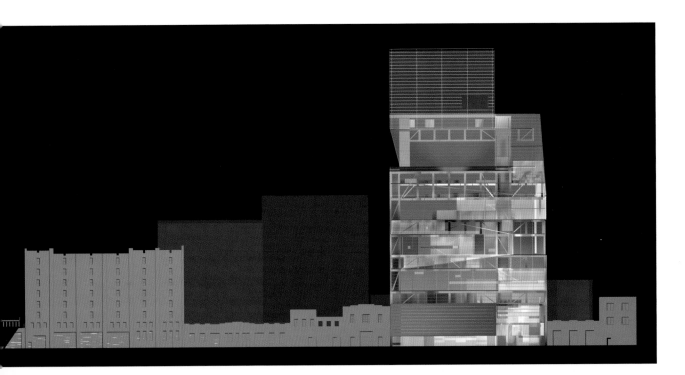

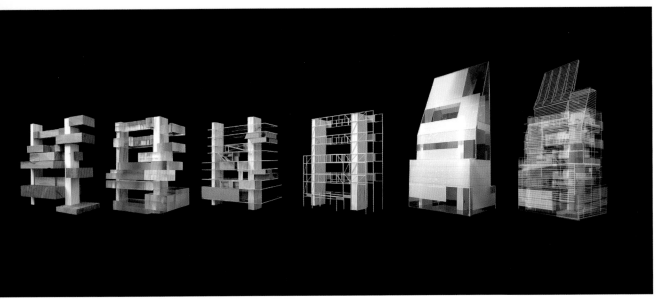

Models: static program, flexible program, circulation, structure, envelope, composite

The Nativity Church, La Primavera
Culiacan, Sinaloa, Mexico

The design of a church must connect a specific place to an infinite understanding. To answer the challenge for a new church at Culiacan, Mexico, we drew upon common local materials and traditions, the characteristics of the site, and local religious observances. During our site visit for this invited competition, we were struck by the stone retaining walls and the variation of their color and geometry—from sharp, split volcanic stone to its smooth, river-washed counterpart. We noticed that the color variation in the stones, alongside the typical whitewashed stucco, formed a perfect complement to the crisp blues and brilliant oranges of Culiacan's sky throughout the day. Our design builds on these local elements of stone, sky, and light to express La Primavera's connection to a broader world and its endless aspirations.

The church finds its place in a natural refuge within an exposed landscape. When Mary and Joseph were unable to find lodgings in the town of Bethlehem, they took shelter in a stable or cave; the Nativity Church's rough exterior shell protects a smooth interior shell, expressing this experience of shelter in an exposed landscape. The nave of the church is anchored to the landscape at one end and to the sky at the other. The church portal frames views of the lake, neighboring Plaza Carlota, and the surrounding hills. The altar's rose window lets in the diffuse light of the northern sky, and each December, the nativity is illuminated by direct sunlight from above, which grows stronger each week as Christmas approaches.

The perspectival succession of bays in a church's nave overcomes scale and distance to transport each parishioner forward into the space of the altar. In a similar manner, the fluid bays of the Nativity Church transport the observer into the scope of the nativity scene, framing a view of the northern sky. The physical reality of the sculpture is projected out into the boundless space of its meaning.

The angular geometry of the dry stone walls projects into the exterior concrete shell, and the gaps between the stones become glazed slots. The interior shell and exterior shell are structurally integrated but functionally distinct. The exterior shields the church from the elements, while the polished interior defines the space of communion.

Concept sketches

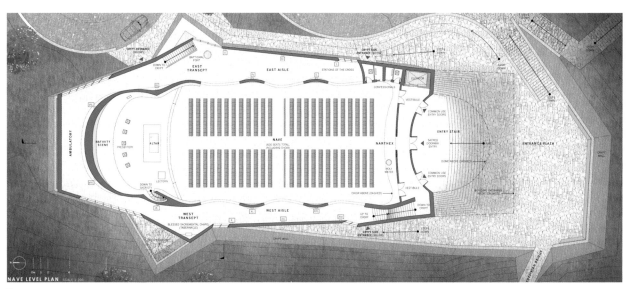

Plan

Model

TRANSVERSAL SECTION · SCALE 1:100

0m 1 2 6 10

Section

LONGITUDINAL SECTION · SCALE 1:100

0m 1 2 6 10

Longitudinal section

One Seventh Avenue South
New York, New York
—

One Seventh Avenue South has commercial space on the ground level and four residential units above. The expanse of glass at the site's 45-degree angle creates an unusual living space with ample views south. We used the rhythm and materiality of the facade to help transition between the industrial loft buildings across the street and the adjacent village townhouses.

Battery Maritime Building Redevelopment
New York, New York
—

We are designing a 140-room boutique hotel with rooftop restaurant and a multiuse food venue at the landmark 1909 Battery Maritime Building. The project has been approved by the Landmarks Preservation Commission; the new addition, with its reflective glass, helps "put back the sky" over the historic structure.

Downtown Tower
New York, New York
—

Our proposal for a commercial, residential, and hotel development in Lower Manhattan is located near the South Street Seaport, along the East River. Inspired by the work of sculptor Fred Sandback, the simple geometry adheres to a dominant vertical line, continuous for the height of the building. As the light changes throughout the day, this strong vertical complements the horizontal plane of the East River.

Gowanus Green
Brooklyn, New York
with West 8 and Starr Whitehouse
—

Our winning proposal for Gowanus Public Place, a brownfield site, features eight residential buildings, ground floor retail, waterfront open space, public parks, a community space, and a boathouse. An integrated landscape and storm water system knits the program together; a series of educational features supports and celebrates the revival of the Gowanus waterfront.

University of Georgia
Lamar Dodd School of Art Master Plan
Athens, Georgia
with Menefee + Winer Architects
—

We were selected to conduct the programming and planning to consolidate the Lamar Dodd School of Art on a new part of campus at the University of Georgia. Fourteen departments and programs will be brought together in a new 210,000-square-foot building, on a hillside site by the Oconee River, where it will join the Georgia Museum of Art, the Performing Arts Center, and the School of Music.

Achievement First Endeavor Charter School
Brooklyn, New York
—

Completed in January 2010, this former factory building was transformed into a new community landmark. The facade materials, windows, and metal-clad entry canopies give the building presence in the neighborhood. The focal point of the new addition to the original building is a precast concrete stair enclosed by colorful wall graphics that are visible through the corner curtain wall. Along with bright open classrooms and science labs, the school includes a skylit cafeteria, a gymnasium, and two rooftop play spaces to achieve a total learning environment.

350 West Broadway
New York, New York
—

We completed the 350 West Broadway project design before the building was sold by the client. The project was to be a new forty-one thousand-square-foot mixed-use development in SoHo. An existing two-story structure was to be renovated and adapted for retail use, while an eleven-story residential tower would be added at its southern end.

South Fork Natural History Museum
Bridgehampton, New York
—

This natural history museum is the trailhead for a system of preserved lands known as the Long Pond Greenbelt, in Bridgehampton, New York. The building is a physical marker at the line between the developed and the undeveloped environment. Using the interstitial space between an existing structure and new construction, the building creates a doorway to the protected lands and illuminates wherever possible the fragile interaction between the developed and vegetal environments.

Adaptations

Pratt Institute, Higgins Hall
Brooklyn, New York

Our work at Higgins Hall, Pratt Institute's School of Architecture, spanned ten years and was an exercise in accident, discovery, and accommodation. What began as a limited investigation into dilapidated conditions became a full renovation and reconstruction when a four-alarm fire consumed the hall's central wing (built in 1868) and left the north wing a gutted masonry shell. We worked with the school to develop a plan for recovery. Programs would temporarily relocate to an underused warehouse space, and we would complete the renovation of the north and south wings.

From the exterior today, the north wing appears to be a well-restored nineteenth-century landmark. The interior reveals a more layered story, with new interventions counterpoised against a historic backdrop. The fire, and the fire fighting, laid Higgins's history bare, leaving evidence of six successive building projects—cast iron columns, bricked-in masonry openings, and curved masonry walls. We incorporated this construction narrative into the renovation, seeking the poetic within the ruin and creating inspiring spaces for learning about architecture within a very limited finishes budget. Orchestrating demolition was key to this process. New openings in the existing masonry's bearing walls create light-filled studio spaces while double-height spaces created by the fire become dramatic review spaces with gallery balconies. The building participates in the teaching of architecture since the tectonics of the original structure and the new interventions are clearly revealed—for example, major pipe runs are gathered into galvanized covers that run along the existing brick walls and structural connections are exposed.

We reconstructed the deteriorating exterior of the south wing using primarily salvaged materials. We reconfigured the roof profile to allow for new operable windows, clerestories, and skylights. The south wing's most dramatic element is a cantilevered, blackened steel stair that completes the original ornate cast-iron stair.

The new construction of the central wing creates an entryway and lobby for the school; all of its mechanical systems are located in the north wing, allowing for maximum light and openness. The central wing was completed last. Steven Holl Architects worked with us on the new entry and glass connector. It negotiates significant floor height differences between the north and south wings with a series of ramps and stairs.

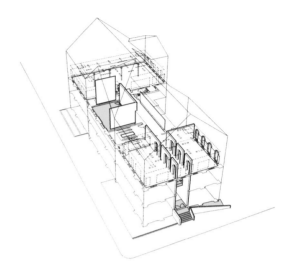

New York Times photo of the damage to the central wing after
the 1996 fire

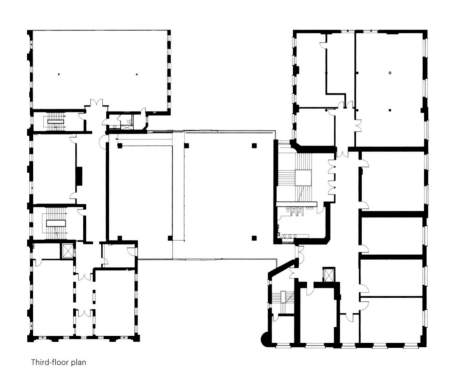

Third-floor plan

The central wing negotiates the significant floor height differences between the north and south wings.

The Studio Museum in Harlem
New York, New York

The great museums in New York have iconographic relationships to the city. The Metropolitan Museum of Art sits on a plinth above a majestic stair. The Whitney is set away from the street by a moat. The Guggenheim is a sculptural object, indifferent to its context. To help the Studio Museum claim its place among these more established giants we looked for its iconic potential, and found a slot. We transformed the 25' x 200' derelict lot adjacent to the museum into its main entry, creating a signature relationship to the city. The slot creates a strong gathering place that increases public presence of the museum. The design responds to the speed and energy of 125th Street with an eddy where pedestrian flow slows down and collects before entering the building.

The Studio Museum's mission is to collect and exhibit art of the African diaspora, representing a dispersed people who are not stylistically similar or geographically linked. The glass facade conveys the open and inclusive attitude central to the museum's goals. During the day, the translucent channels create a visual calm that focuses attention through the transparent glass window into the museum lobby. At night, when the heavy metal shutters of the neighboring retail shops are drawn, the facade glows and becomes a magnet for activity.

The slot's courtyard is bracketed by tapered figures, one of glass and the other of stone, that orchestrate egress stairs, mechanical systems, and light. The glass tower draws light to the lower levels and accentuates the vertical procession down to the main gallery spaces below. Inside, natural light directs the sequential exploration of the space, providing visual cues for where to go next.

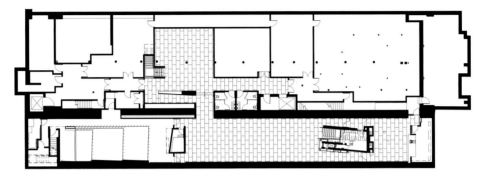

Upper-floor plan

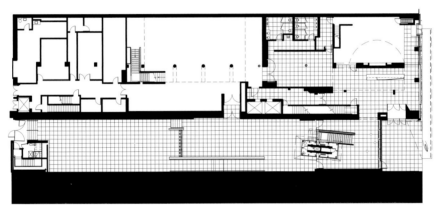

Ground-floor plan

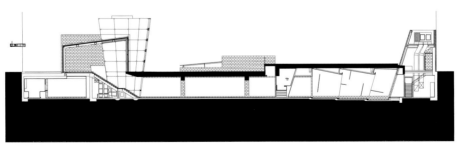

Section

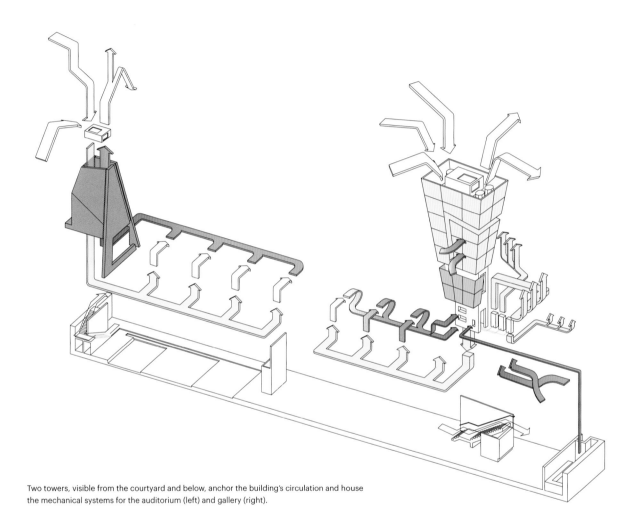

Two towers, visible from the courtyard and below, anchor the building's circulation and house
the mechanical systems for the auditorium (left) and gallery (right).

St. John's Bread & Life
Brooklyn, New York

From its home in New York's Bedford-Stuyvesant neighborhood, St. John's Bread & Life soup kitchen provides daily meals to over one thousand people a day. The building houses a dining hall and food pantry as well as literacy classes, job placement programs, legal assistance, and medical services. On a very limited budget we sought to create a building that supports Bread & Life's mission of "feeding mind, body, and spirit" by making the most of existing features and employing a limited number of architectural moves.

The plan is organized so that patrons drawn to the popular food programs will also come into contact with the center's other services. For example, the library offering résumé and job search assistance is placed along the facade adjacent to the entrance and across from the dining hall. Just beyond the entry lobby, a skylighted court brings natural light deep into the warehouse floor plate and organizes Bread & Life's other services: food pantry, teaching kitchen, classroom, chapel on the ground floor, and offices for one-on-one help on the second floor. A second skylight brings natural light to the second-floor meeting room and turns Sheetrock into an inspirational metaphor in the chapel's sweeping ceiling.

Making the most of existing materials and features stretched the construction budget and reinforced Bread & Life's philosophy of respect and dignity for people. We highlighted the ad hoc structure that the warehouse developed over time with a simple grid of light fixtures. We refinished the existing joists that were removed to make the skylights and used them to create the chapel wall and the reception desk. The plain brick walls and the palette of glass, steel, wood, and concrete create a symbolic harmony between the traditional aspects of the community and the progressive social work of the client.

The former warehouse

The dining room, a popular draw, is visible from the street at right of the entrance. Patrons who come for meals can also take advantage of services like the resource library.

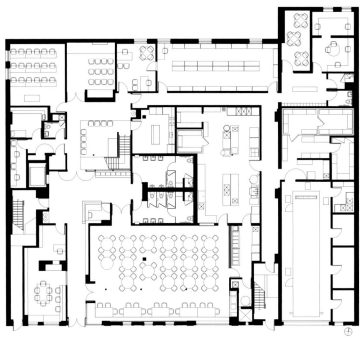

Ground-floor plan

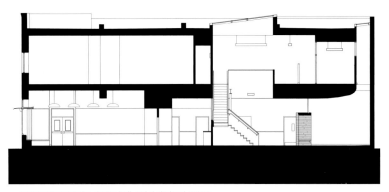

Section through the dining hall and skylighted atrium

New York Public Library, Mulberry Street Branch
New York, New York

How could our project entice pedestrians into the subterranean spaces of a former chocolate factory, some forty-five feet below grade? Although this task may have been an easy one for a confectionary predecessor, it was a formidable challenge for the new Mulberry Street branch of the New York Public Library in SoHo. The library's street presence would be limited to a small side-street entry. A few design interventions addressed multiple issues. We worked with New York's Department of Transportation to ramp up the existing sidewalk thirty inches to meet the existing first-floor level, providing ADA-compliant access and letting us bring light and air into the lower level. The city physically responds to the presence of the library. Fresh air enters through the canopy, and spill air leaves under the ramp. At night the void under the ramp is illuminated, and the entry reads as a floating plane above the street level.

The library's constituency is widely varied, from elderly residents looking for a place to read the paper to young kids looking for computer access and homework help. Our goal was to encourage all users to experience the pleasure of wandering in a world of knowledge. An architectural "bookworm" weaves through the space, starting as a canopy over the entry and transforming into a soffit over the winding central stair, organizing mechanical systems and lighting as it travels to the lower-level collections and the children's, young adult, and adult reading rooms. The bookworm guides patrons through the collections and leads them back out of the labyrinth.

The existing timber floor structure, cast-iron columns, and brick walls provided a warm, historic palette against which we played contemporary materials and fixtures. A reclaimed beam became a desk for computer terminals; access doors to former furnaces were refinished and left exposed.

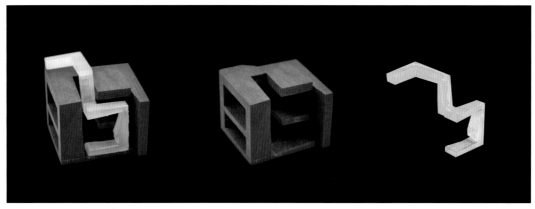

Stair to the cellar and subcellar. The ribbon "bookworm" above organizes building systems and guides visitors through the space.

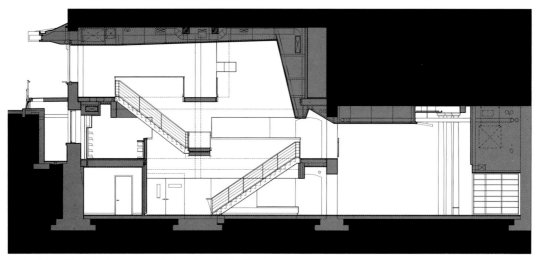

Section. Most of the library's programs are in the cellar and subcellar levels.

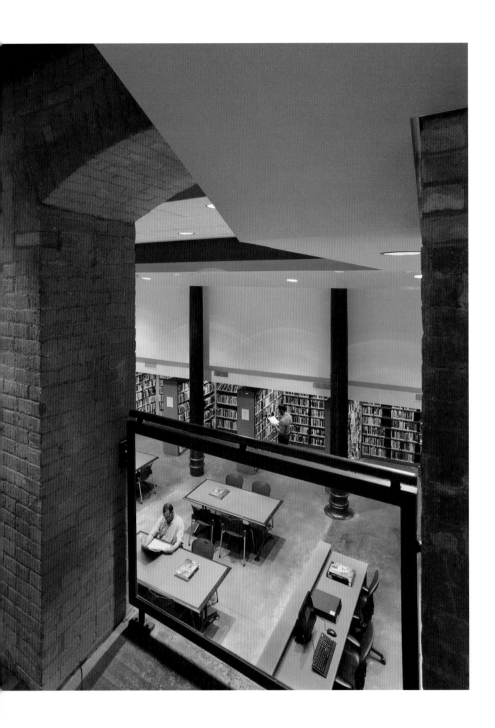

Theory Headquarters
New York, New York

We wanted Theory's new headquarters in Manhattan's Meatpacking District to add to the distinctive character of this neighborhood, with its combination of active nightlife and daytime industry. The project occupies five floors of a new building at the corner of Greenwich and Gansevoort Streets. For the ground-floor flagship retail space, we drew from local materials—steel hooks, concrete, street art, butcher block—and combined them with velvet, leather, polished acrylic, and lacquer to create an environment that reflected the brand and the site. The district's once-ubiquitous steel hooks and rails, used to hang and convey meat, are the inspiration for the sliding ceiling-hung clothing racks that allow the space to be easily reconfigured. Hickory wood floor fixtures on casters create an accessories market at the center of the space. A dynamic combination of raw and luxe is evident in the clothing as well as the architecture.

The company's showrooms, workrooms, and offices animate the floors above. A new central stair set in an elongated open slot carries natural light from a walkable skylight above through the core of the building, weaving together the company's departments. Rather than a conventional switchback configuration, each flight of the stair faces onto the flight below, making the most of spontaneous employee interaction. The stair's precast concrete treads contrast with polished stainless steel stanchions and a low-iron glass guardrail, held in a cap custom designed to fit the hand— the tactile and visual experience leading the eye, the hand, and the foot up through the building. Two four-story panels of woven stainless steel hang at the north side of the stair, bringing reflected light deep into the building during the day and highlighting the connection between multiple floors. The panels are richly illuminated at night, reinforcing the company's unified identity from the exterior.

Natural light reaches the central work areas through a permeable perimeter of offices and workspaces. All partitions float independently, creating maximum openings for light and view. Doors are full-height and oversized, providing privacy when needed but typically left open, encouraging exchange.

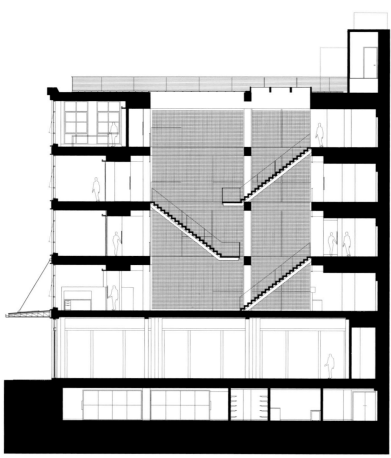

Section through the stair

Ground-floor retail space

Canal Street Residence
New York, New York
—

This project repurposes an old paper factory floor and adds a new penthouse and roof terrace. We used light to create connections between the renovated existing floor and the new spaces above. Light enters the three-level stair and filters through glass treads; a strip of light continues around the perimeter of the living space. Sculptural skylights appear on the terrace as objects in fields of tall grasses.

Kate Spade Shops Worldwide
—

We have worked with accessories brand Kate Spade on their domestic and international retail spaces for over fifteen years. For this shop, we screened the existing faux-Tudor building so that it is almost concealed during the day and dramatically accented at night.

29th Street Penthouse
New York, New York
—

This penthouse for a European artist and collector in New York's flower district was conceived as a clean foil for the client's collection of art and furniture, which now includes a custom fourteen-foot French Racing Blue table we designed to recall his 1960s Peugeot convertible.

Tanya Bonakdar Gallery
New York, New York
—

We took this old taxi garage and converted it into a contemporary art gallery; the exhibit space is located on the second floor. An inviting transition in the form of a pine and blackened steel stair entices visitors to enter from the street. We refurbished existing skylights and exposed building structure to increase the apparent scale of the space.

McCarren Pool Redevelopment
Brooklyn, New York

—

We are designing the restoration of the 1936 landmark McCarren Pool, constructed by Fiorello LaGuardia and Robert Moses. The project reactivates an existing outdoor pool and provides space for ice skating in winter months. An indoor recreation and community center will occupy the historic bathhouse and be open year-round.

Ninth Street Residence
New York, New York

—

We combined two postwar apartments, former Sheetrock boxes with low ceilings and an underused terrace. Enclosing the living room with industrial channel glass, this addition draws light into the interior of the apartment throughout the day. At night the living room glows through its translucent glass walls and acts as a large-scale lantern.

145 Hudson Street
New York, New York
with James Carpenter Design Associates

—

A 140,000-square-foot former printing factory in historic Tribeca was transformed into a mixed-use commercial and residential building. On the upper floors, twenty-one new luxury loft condominiums take advantage of spectacular light and both city and river views. After an extensive review by the Landmarks Preservation Commission, we added a ten thousand-square-foot duplex penthouse, sheathed in glass, with a 360-degree view of Lower Manhattan. Mullions, parapets, and stairs, all made of glass, reinforce the transparency and luminosity of the space, inside and out.

Tom Wesselmann Studio
New York, New York

—

Designed in collaboration with the painter, this working studio incorporates galleries, museum-quality archival storage, and work areas on three floors of a loft building. The space is designed around a ribbon-shaped wall for viewing the progress of individual pieces within a series. Custom designed with the artist, light fixtures meet his preference to make and view his paintings. Office and storage space occupies the second floor with a minimal row of natural light on one side to preserve the light below. The long, open loft studio is designed to ultimately transform into a museum for the artist's work.

Public Spaces

The Elevated Acre at 55 Water Street
New York, New York
with Ken Smith Landscape Architects

People like to meet the water's edge. This universal truth, as put by Herman Melville, inspired our winning entry in this international competition for a new park atop a parking garage.

Located between a seventy-five-story tower and fifteen-story trading floor annex both designed by Emery Roth, the site is a classic example of a privately owned public space, made available through an exchange of building height for open space. Like many of these spaces, the existing plaza was not evident to pedestrians as a public space. We wanted to transform the windswept concrete hardscape into a multiprogrammed and accessible public park that affords a year-round connection to the water often lost in this neighborhood, despite its proximity to the East River. A relentless concrete stair had provided access to the thirty-foot-high site; we replaced it with illuminated new escalators and stairs punctuated with seating, sculptural glass elements, and planted outcroppings. Upon entering the park, a visitor can get a private bench amidst tall grasses or lounge on the large event lawn. A boardwalk edge offers panoramic views of the Brooklyn Bridge and Governors Island.

A steel and glass beacon anchors the park's northeast corner. The tower includes event support space and serves as a welcoming lantern to the highway and harbor. The beacon recalls a lost historic site element, the Titanic Memorial Lighthouse. The custom designed glass and stainless steel structure allowed us to set glass panels anywhere within a three-inch tolerance, providing a textured surface off of which natural and artificial light play. LED strips provide a range of colors for special events and holidays. Together, the park elements recall the glacial landscape of Long Island, with its terminal moraines, eskers, and escarpments, offering textures and forms rarely available in an urban setting.

The competition boards

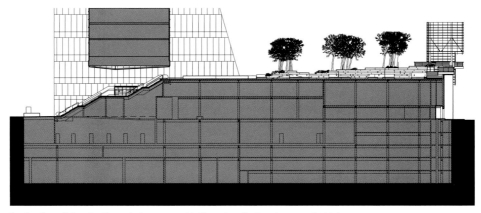

Section through the site. The park slopes upward to the water, allowing views over the highway.

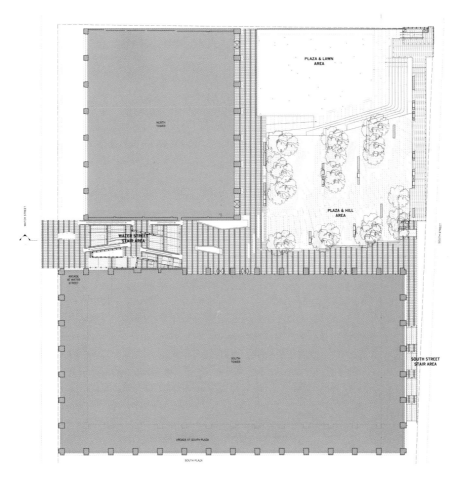

Site plan

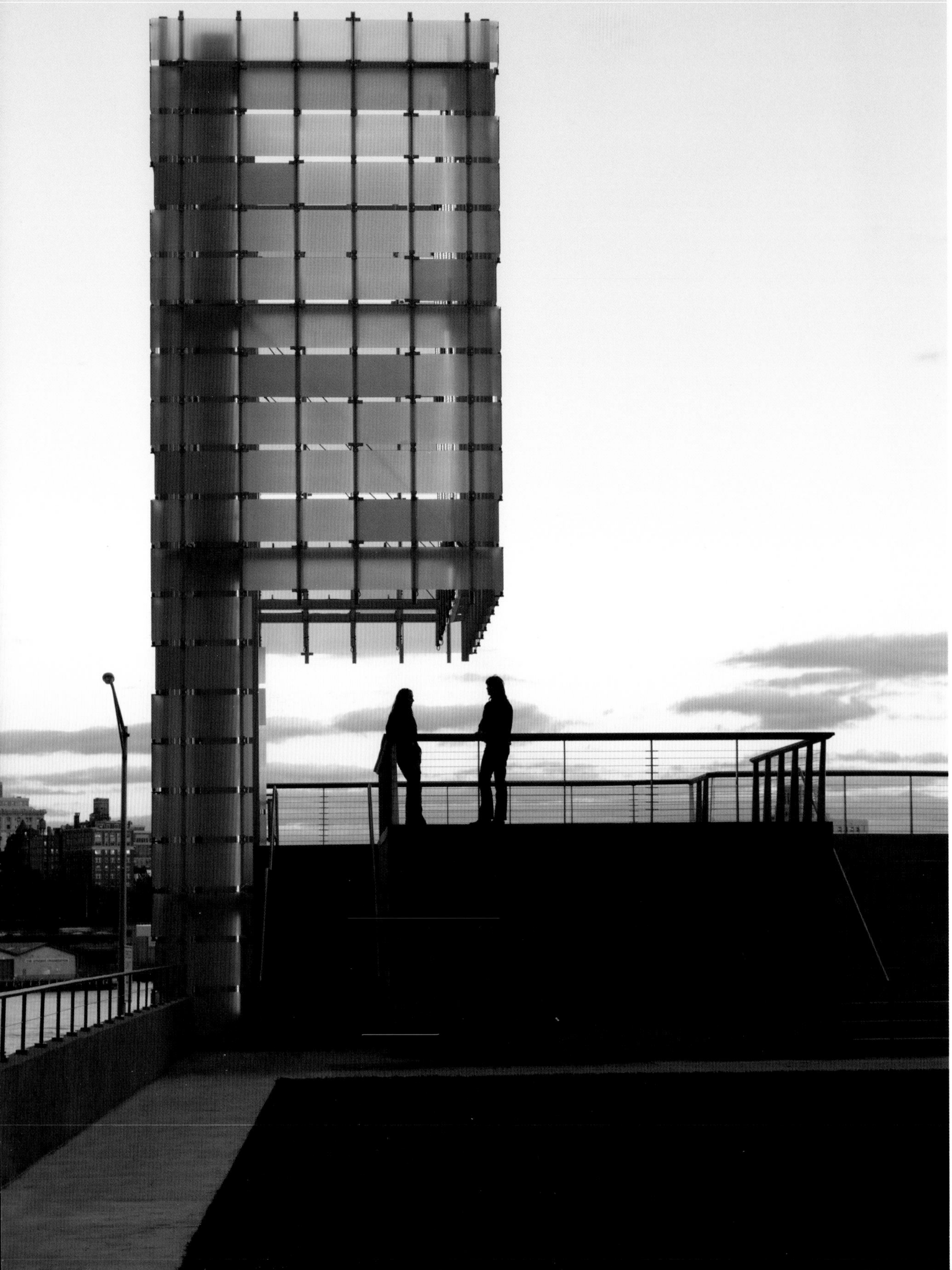

The structure allows each panel of glass to be installed within a three-inch tolerance, giving the facade a subtle texture.

Planters and glowing glass panels anticipate the beacon.

**New York Stock Exchange Financial District
Security and Streetscapes**
New York, New York
with Quennell Rothschild and Partners

Immediately after the attacks of September 11, 2001, the City of New York and the New York Stock Exchange (NYSE) secured its perimeter, suddenly viewed as a prime target. They installed Jersey barriers, manned checkpoints, mobile vehicular interdiction devices, and other off-the-shelf equipment to create a safe standoff distance between the Exchange and unscreened pedestrians and vehicles. These temporary measures felt all too permanent after two years. Visually and physically intrusive, they were devastating to area businesses and unsettling for property owners, residents, and visitors. The neighborhood felt constantly under siege.

In the summer of 2003 the Department of City Planning asked us to lead the design team for security and streetscape enhancements throughout the Financial District. Our challenge was to provide protection for one of the world's most important financial markets while also improving the pedestrian experience in one of the densest parts of Manhattan. Narrow streets with a tangled thicket of infrastructure just below grade, combined with the landmark status of the surrounding buildings, created physical constraints. Multiple government entities with overlapping jurisdictional powers held a stake in the site, further complicating the project.

We asked ourselves if the things that provide security could also be the things that make people want to stay. We designed a series of custom devices for key locations, working with the U.S. Army Corps of Engineers and the NYPD to meet security requirements while focusing on keeping views open and public space accessible. The sculptural NoGo bollard, a crystalline bronze form, uses light and shadow to reduce its apparent mass. Passersby and children enjoy them as a place to sit and lean. For locations where security devices would not fit amidst the underground utilities, we developed shallow-foundation barriers. Perforated bronze lanterns attached to a turntable look friendly and keep view corridors unblocked. These elements were deployed as part of an urban design strategy that re-engineered traffic flows and moved vehicle security check-points away from major pedestrian zones. We reintroduced the district's historic cobble paving and inlaid blocks of end-grain wood to recall the wood posts of Wall Street's historic namesake. Curb inscriptions give a history of the Broad Street Canal, buried in 1676, inspiring passersby to reflect on the growth of the city and this district.

Section of Wall Street palisade

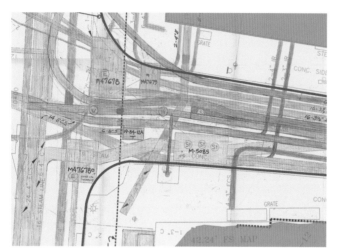

Sub-grade infrastructure

Pre-design conditions

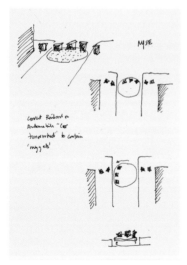

The turntable rotates to allow cars to pass
while keeping view corridors open.

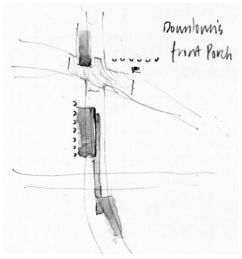

Concept sketch

Unitized cobbles

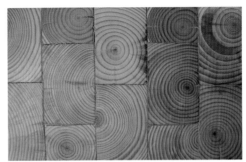

Wood inlay at line of original palisade

Full-scale crash test at the Texas Transportation Institute

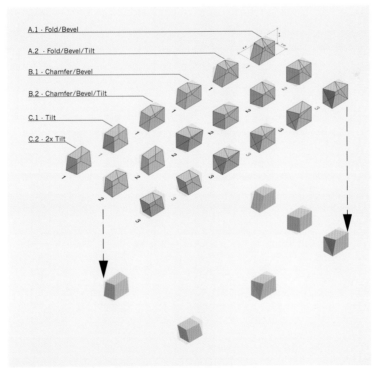

A.1 · Fold/Bevel

A.2 · Fold/Bevel/Tilt

B.1 · Chamfer/Bevel

B.2 · Chamfer/Bevel/Tilt

C.1 · Tilt

C.2 · 2x Tilt

Iterative studies for the NoGo bollard

Perforated bronze lanterns rotate to allow authorized traffic to pass.
The bronze is durable and requires little maintenance.

Battery Park City Streetscapes
New York, New York
with James Carpenter Design Associates

Battery Park City, adjacent to the World Trade Center site, was in tremendous
need of pedestrian and neighborhood amenities after 9/11. It also required
an integrated plan for protecting the perimeter of the financial institutions that
form the district's commercial core, including the New York Mercantile
Exchange and American Express. The Battery Park City Authority asked us to
redesign their streetscapes to meet these seemingly incompatible goals.

Our design team studied threat vectors for high- and low-speed approaches
to specific buildings to determine appropriate levels of protection. Although
vehicular threats are often studied using general assumptions and resolved
with commonly applied arrest techniques, this design responds to the specific
movements and capabilities within a restricted urban environment. We also
negotiated a Cooperative Research and Development Agreement (CRADA) with
the U.S. Army Corps of Engineers to study and test immobilization techniques
for a variety of vehicle arrest assemblies.

The design team studied the neighborhood context, realizing that the
installation of security measures would dramatically alter the nature
of pedestrian and public space. The desire for security had to be balanced
with a need to maintain a quality of life and public space for both visitors
and residents of Battery Park City. Numerous urban issues were reviewed in
combination with security requirements in order to synthesize a common
solution.

Traffic calming measures such as raised crosswalks and narrowed inter-
sections allow for both safer pedestrian passage and forced vehicle slowdown.
Glowing glass benches stretch the length of Vesey Street between the new
ferry terminal and the proposed Freedom Tower, providing wayfinding and
rest for pedestrians. The benches are combined with a compressible fill
"tiger trap" to act as an anti-ram barrier. The compressible fill allows the barrier
wall to be partially submerged and act much taller than its aboveground profile
suggests. Pedestrians and bicycles can walk atop the fill as any sidewalk, but
the weight of a vehicle will fall into the fill and be stopped at the barrier wall.

This glowing axis is crossed by the steel and specialty glass shade structures
on North End Avenue, which provides shade in the daytime and reflected
light at night. The structures mark new amenities including a dog run, a plant
nursery, and a picnic lawn.

A quarter mile of lit benches will connect the ferry terminal to the Freedom Tower. Intersecting axes of canopies, marking public amenities and a security checkpoint, help define the district.

Compressible fill used in the Battery Park project was engineered to stop airplanes that overtravel their runway.

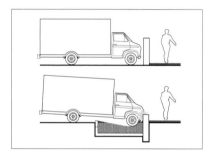

The compressible fill allows sunken barrier walls to sit at bench height above ground.

The streetscape concept: a five-foot-wide trench (typical for street trees) with compressible fill that can accommodate canopies, seating, and plantings. The security measure is invisible to the pedestrian.

Governors Island Park and Public Space Competition
New York, New York
with West 8

In December 2007, a design team led by West 8 and Rogers Marvel Architects was chosen as the winner of the international design competition for Governors Island. The island, once languishing in relative isolation, is to become an exploration in recreating paradise. A combination of natural and crafted landscapes will conjure up fantasies of a lost utopia—of nature, the primordial, and of artificial worlds—creating an unimaginably diverse visual experience along the Hudson shoreline.

The existing island is made up of two distinct landscapes; the north island with its natural topography and historic buildings, and the flat south island built on subway tunnel fill and dotted with obsolete buildings slated for demolition. While the landscape structure of the north was established, the landscape of the south island had to be invented. In contrast to Central Park, where the street grid frames the park, for Governors Island, the park geometry was to be dominant. Starting from the gateway of Liggett Hall, which forms the threshold between the north and south of the island, the park's geometry extends out across the south island, defining paths and topography but also shaping the development zones at its perimeter. Its intensity rises as it stretches away from the historic island, culminating in the hilly Vertical Landscape installation—a green foil for the Manhattan skyline.

In our entry, five key destinations within the park allow for a wealth of spaces and activities: the North Island Historic District Open Space, the Great Lawn, the Great Promenade, the Vertical Landscape, and the Marsh. Visitors will wander the boardwalks, promenades, and sinuous paths, using free, sustainable wooden bikes to discover unforgettable views of the Statue of Liberty and to explore the island's many introduced biotypes.

The Vertical Landscape, developed in part from a distortion of the city grid, will be built from recycled materials taken from the island itself. Relocated earth fill and debris from the eroding buildings will construct "hills" that house various programs and provide panoramic views. Steeped in the natural and cultural history of the New York Harbor, Governors Island will re-emerge as the next great world park, becoming a global exemplar of sustainability, a beacon for the harbor, and an icon for the city.

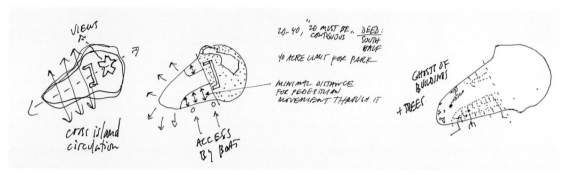

Concept sketch

The new park is in the south, below the historic district.

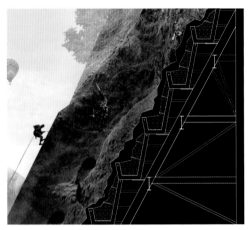

Construction concept for the new hills

A constructed playscape

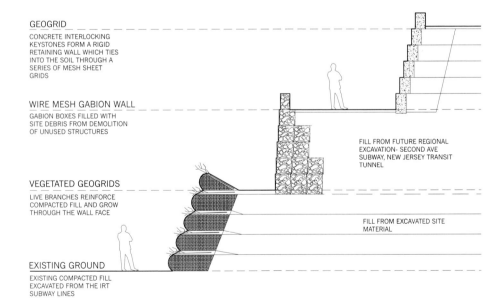

GEOGRID

CONCRETE INTERLOCKING
KEYSTONES FORM A RIGID
RETAINING WALL WHICH TIES
INTO THE SOIL THROUGH A
SERIES OF MESH SHEET
GRIDS

WIRE MESH GABION WALL

GABION BOXES FILLED WITH
SITE DEBRIS FROM DEMOLITION
OF UNUSED STRUCTURES

FILL FROM FUTURE REGIONAL
EXCAVATION- SECOND AVE
SUBWAY, NEW JERSEY TRANSIT
TUNNEL

VEGETATED GEOGRIDS

LIVE BRANCHES REINFORCE
COMPACTED FILL AND GROW
THROUGH THE WALL FACE

FILL FROM EXCAVATED SITE
MATERIAL

EXISTING GROUND

EXISTING COMPACTED FILL
EXCAVATED FROM THE IRT
SUBWAY LINES

Proposed cross section through the engineered hills

Metropolitan Tower
New York, New York

Our client asked us to renovate their public through-block lobby to create a more inviting, recognizable entrance to the commercial segment of the building. This privately owned public space was originally created in return for additional buildable area beyond what the zoning resolution would typically allow. This public space function means that the lobby has 24-hour public access. We wanted the lobby to play off the existing building rather than appear as a lobby renovation. People should feel invited and welcomed, the concierge and elevator areas should create a sense of arrival, and the lobby should function effectively in both its public and private roles.

We covered the lobby's interior walls with black aluminum panels similar in proportion to the exterior glass to relate it to the building envelope, which appears to fold into the lobby, creating a seamless transition into the space. The reveals in the panels align with those of the granite floor, creating a cohesive whole. At wall openings, the panels fold and taper to meet the existing lobby structure. Indirect cove light, the main light source, creates a warm ambient glow. The concierge desk is a color-changing, back-lit glass box that creates a destination point for visitors, while, opposite the desk, a continuous video-screen strip runs the length of the public passage, helping to draw people into the building from the sidewalk. This changing public art display features a range of artists and acknowledges the lobby's role as public space.

The biggest design challenge was to create a fully functioning public passageway while also maintaining a designated lobby space. The public and private functions of the space had to be clearly defined while still reading as one space. Lighting was our key tool: the linear lighting guides pedestrians through the lobby, highlighting the public space. The beacon of light provided by the lobby desk clearly identifies the private space without obstructing the pedestrian pathway.

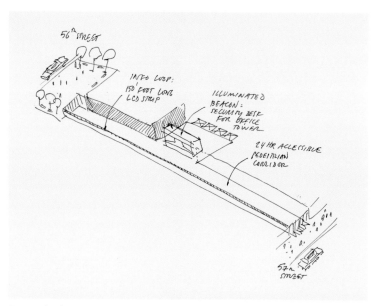

Concept sketch

Earlier schemes for the passage

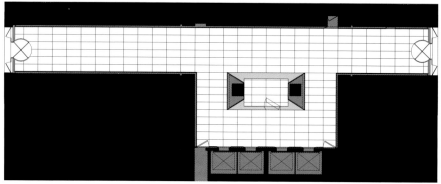

Plan

Dwight D. Eisenhower Memorial Competition
Washington, DC
with Nelson Byrd Woltz Landscape Architects and Arup

The team lead by Rogers Marvel Architects was one of four finalists in the U.S. General Service Administration's Dwight D. Eisenhower Memorial Commission competition to design the new Eisenhower memorial just off the National Mall in Washington, DC. The new memorial will sit on a four-acre site south of Independence Avenue in front of the Department of Education.

Our entry celebrates the legacy of both public service and public space in a three stage narrative: at the Entry Pavilion, Ike is the barefoot boy turned soldier; at The Crossing, the Supreme Commander leads the men; and in the Leadership Pavilion, the President quietly guides the world. By representing Eisenhower's deeds the memorial expresses the nation's democratic ideals. Visitors ascend through the Stepped Lawn, the tall grass of the American Prairie, and a thirteen-striped Regimented Grove to arrive at the central water crossing and the crisp marble pavilions. They pause to contemplate in the Sentinel Garden, turn to see newly framed views of the city, and leave with recognition of the value of public service.

Washington's open spaces are defined by intersecting diagonal avenues and orthogonal streets. The Eisenhower Memorial redefines these spaces by creating infinite vanishing points that address the evolving American urban landscape.

The project was a close collaboration between Rogers Marvel Architects, landscape architects Nelson Byrd Woltz, information designers Local Projects, lighting designer George Sexton Associates, and engineers Arup. We proposed landscapes taken from Eisenhower's life: Kansas prairie, Normandy shores, and Washington's Mall; and we explored how to use technology to allow a visitor's experience to extend beyond the confines of the site, without creating a place that would be outdated almost immediately. No technology is built-in. All media interventions are formless strategies, like a radio station that motorists pick up when they are stuck in traffic, that will evolve with the decades.

The Sentinel Garden: a place to reflect before returning to the realm of the city.

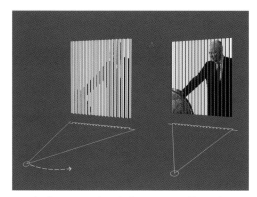

Outside of a certain angle, only the texture is visible. As the viewer approaches the specific perspective, the image appears.

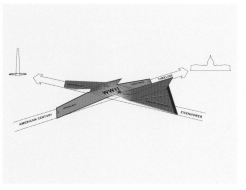

Crossing axes of the twentieth-century world and Eisenhower's life

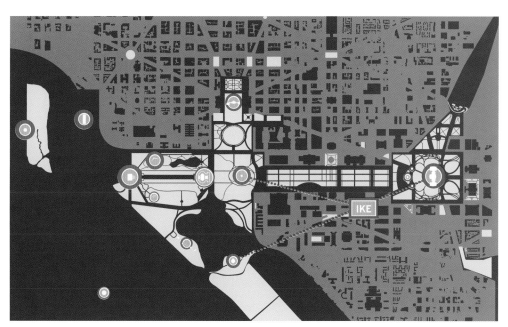

Washington's monuments, seen together, tell the story of our nation.

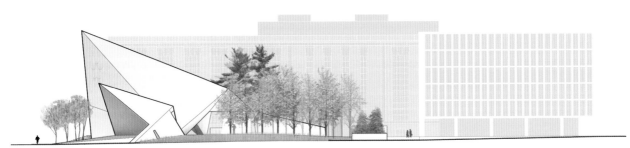

West elevation

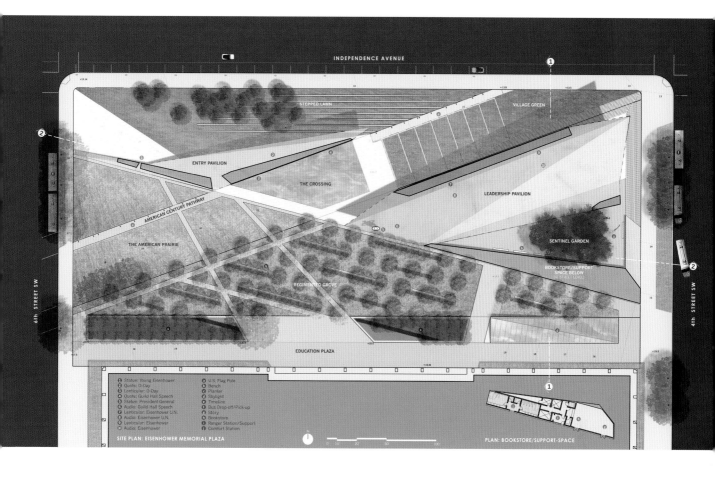

INDEPENDENCE AVENUE

STEPPED LAWN

VILLAGE GREEN

ENTRY PAVILION

THE CROSSING

LEADERSHIP PAVILION

AMERICAN CENTURY PATHWAY

THE AMERICAN PRAIRIE

SENTINEL GARDEN

BOOKSTORE/SUPPORT
SPACE BELOW

REGIMENTED GROVE

6th STREET SW

4th STREET SW

EDUCATION PLAZA

1. Statue: Young Eisenhower
2. Quote: D-Day
3. Lenticular: D-Day
4. Quote: Guild Hall Speech
5. Statue: President General
6. Audio: Guild Hall Speech
7. Lenticular: Eisenhower U.N.
8. Audio: Eisenhower U.N.
9. Lenticular: Eisenhower
10. Audio: Eisenhower

- U.S. Flag Pole
- Bench
- Planter
- Skylight
- Timeline
- Bus Drop-off/Pick-up
- Story
- Bookstore
- Ranger Station/Support
- Comfort Station

SITE PLAN: EISENHOWER MEMORIAL PLAZA

PLAN: BOOKSTORE/SUPPORT-SPACE

East elevation

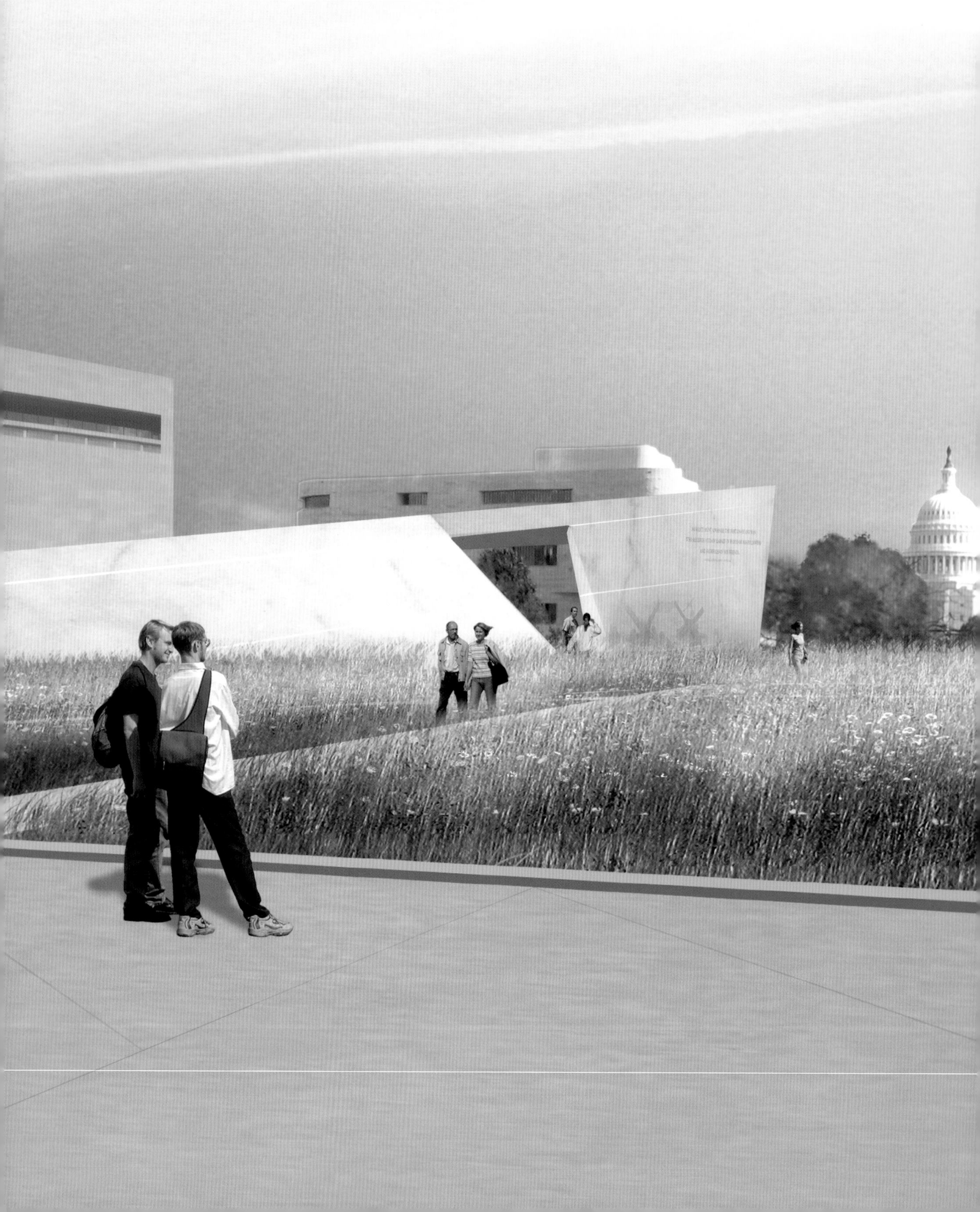

Pentagon South Plaza
Arlington, Virginia
with Ritter Architects
—

The U.S. Department of Defense hired us to implement a portion of the Pentagon Reservation master plan. The scope includes the design of a new pedestrian plaza to convey visitors and workers into the primary pedestrian entrance of the Pentagon. Through extensive research into the history of military land-scape fortifications, the design team identified methods for converting historic military earthwork typologies into modern security strategies relevant to the Pentagon campus.

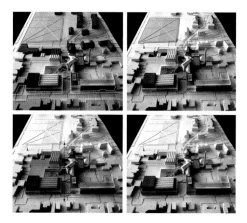

Dartmouth College Arts Master Plan
Hanover, New Hampshire
—

We developed a comprehensive master plan for the expanding arts facilities at Dartmouth College. The arts center becomes a threshold between the pastoral space of the campus and the commercial environment of the town. A string of green weaves through it, connecting the buildings of the complex to the town and the campus. The plan acknowledges the importance of green spaces on campus by preserving existing courtyards and proposing new ones.

MTA Flood Mitigation Furniture and Urban Plan
Queens, New York
with di Domenico + Partners
—

The MTA retained us as part of a team to protect the subway from a hundred-year storm, despite having storm sewers designed for a two- to five-year storm. The project addresses flood-prone areas in Queens with a modular solution that can be applied to other areas. Established by a hydrological study that marks the minute topographical distinctions that shape the flood, the undulating form of these raised grates responds to the varied depths of expected flooding, emulating the flooding that the grates help solve.

Times Square Streetscape
New York, New York
—

Reconciling infrastructure and public space is often the focus of our work. For the Times Square Alliance, we developed a streetscape design that integrates the unique pedestrian experience in Times Square with a high volume of traffic, allowing the space to adapt to peak vehicle and peak pedestrian operation.

SandRidge Energy
Oklahoma City, Oklahoma
with Hoerr Schaudt Landscape Architects

—

The SandRidge Energy project encompasses multiple downtown blocks, weaving architecture and landscape architecture to strike a balance between company needs and civic engagement. The master plan responds to the city's challenging climate of high street-level winds by proposing an "outdoor interior" that links the buildings on the site and enables employees and the community to enjoy a vibrant landscape of native eco-regions in an urban environment.

Nathan Phillips Square Design Competition
Toronto, Canada
with Ken Smith Landscape Architect and du Toit Allsop Hillier

—

This finalist design expands the square to engage its surroundings and improves its functionality with street-level hardscape while activating the upper level with landscape. Roof gardens introduce native planting and link upper and lower spaces with a wooded hill, topped with a tree grove that looks onto the plaza's restaurants, boutiques, and performance spaces. A fritted-glass ribbon at the face of the hill provides a screened shelter from winter winds and hot sun. The consolidation of support spaces under the hill frees the plaza to accommodate public events.

New York 2106
The City of the Future: Design and Engineering Challenge
Sponsored by the History Channel

—

The New York of 2106 must accommodate a 50 percent increase in population, but most of the city's infrastructural networks have reached their capacity. Adding new layers of centralized infrastructure would be prohibitively expensive and increase the burden on disadvantaged neighborhoods. In response to this challenge, we propose a new organization of urban infrastructure built on the sustainable street. By building sustainable infrastructure on a neighborhood scale, the city can grow without increasing its load on metropolitan infrastructure or its impact on the environment.

Erie Street Plaza
Milwaukee, Wisconsin
with Hoerr Schaudt Landscape Architects

—

The Erie Street Plaza in Milwaukee is a hinge. For bikers, joggers, fishermen, and canoeists, it is the threshold between the urban intensity of the River Walk and the openness of the lake. The Erie Street Plaza marks the moment of transition from the Milwaukee and Kinnickinnic rivers to Lake Michigan. Likewise, it is the point where the energy of the city's lakefront path system wraps around, turns inland, and meets the river. This site is an important moment in the city; our finalist design celebrates and exaggerates it.

Jonathan Marvel grew up in Puerto Rico and studied at Dartmouth College and Harvard's Graduate School of Design (GSD). Rob Rogers grew up in Colorado, studied at Rice, and later attended the GSD as well, although they did not meet there. Despite their geographic history, both have made New York City home. Working in the office of I. M. Pei (Rogers) and Richard Meier (Marvel) brought them here, but the work of neither office lead linearly to what Rogers and Marvel do together today.

One cannot help but associate the work of Rogers Marvel Architects with New York City, despite the fact that they work all over the United States. Their willingness to take on unattractive elements of the city, like subway grates and security bollards, further impresses the idea that their work is not just in New York but of New York; not just of New York but intrinsically—and physically—connected to the essence of New York: the high/the low, the iconic/the anonymous, and the expensive/the cheap.

Rogers Marvel Architects makes what I call a new urban vernacular, an architecture that builds out from recognizable forms of the city and adds a new detail, a subtle flair, a much-needed knowing wink. Of course our stock exchange needs to be protected from car bombs, but why not perforate and tickle the surface of a disappearing, dancing traffic stopper. Of course our subways need to breathe and be protected from storm-water flooding, but why not undulate and animate a grating and make it a bench and a bike rack too? Of course cabbies need to rest and stretch, so why not propose their traffic island have a fence that allows stretching, resting, and shaded seating in iconic taxicab yellow to encourage a healthy break outdoors? Creative common sense gives energy to the work of Rogers Marvel Architects. I find it works as a reminder that community identity can take all kinds of forms, and that basing place-bound identity on practical concerns is not an ordinary move but an enlightened one. When I look at their designs for McCarren Pool or 55 Water Street, I see spaces that beget spirited inhabitation, places that allow unbothered relaxation and encourage intrigued interaction depending on the day, the mood of the user, and the ambience of a larger event.

There is an optimism about what urban life can be in what they do. The public spaces shaped and furnished by Rogers Marvel Architects embody that delicious friction between the practical and the exotic. Their work has concrete definitive characteristics, it is serious work but it makes you smile. It is an elegant architecture that is often infused with whimsy and a sense of humor. In New York City, as in everywhere, this is a good thing.

In 2009, Rogers Marvel Architects was named one of four finalists for the Dwight D. Eisenhower Memorial Commission's design competition for an Eisenhower Memorial in Washington, DC. Rumor has it that the jury felt the RMA scheme was "too much architecture" for the four-acre site; Frank Gehry was named the winner. But as a young firm, RMA was a winner nonetheless, breaking a certain invisible barrier to compete with well-known, older architects on a national stage and establishing their presence as the next generation.

The often overwhelming presence of both buildings and architects has been an issue in the age of signature architecture— the age in which RMA, established in 1992, has grown up. Given their backgrounds, it seems both paradoxical and wise that, even after their many combined years of practice, RMA's work focuses on the subtle and the small, even if it means a certain lack of presence or exposure.

In early September 2009, as the recession-spooked stock market flailed, President Obama came to Wall Street to address the New York Stock Exchange. That same day, I unwittingly brought a visiting friend to Wall Street simply to show her the historic streets of New York. Throngs of curiosity seekers and myriad television crews clogged the street, and watchful police standing two and three deep stood guard at the Exchange's entrances. But they had help: sculptural bronze NoGo barriers, which RMA designed for the Stock Exchange in response to the need for heightened security after 9/11.

Beginning in the 1990s, terrorist attacks on buildings in the United States created a surge in demand for exterior security measures. The initial response was the installation of ugly and unthoughtful bollards, planters, and temporary fencing, largely done without consulting architects. When RMA was asked to design a security and streetscape program for the New York Financial District, they not only met the need for barriers but also produced an environment that celebrates the very being and history of the place without inserting a new architectural presence. Only the careful observer would note that the sculptural forms that line the street, or in some instances close off a thoroughfare, are not an installation reminiscent of Isamu Noguchi or of crystals found in nature, but are artfully positioned barriers to vehicular traffic. Two industrial turntables combined with a row of illuminated impact posts can be rotated to give vehicles passage through Wall Street. Scattered among the cobblestone pavers are wood blocks that mark the outline of a historic seventeenth-century stockade, legends carved into curbstones denote historic dates and events. But none of these things, either together or as individual gestures, calls out "architecture." Each detail is there simply to be discovered by the passerby or the lingering New Yorker showing a visitor the city.

The Financial District project is a clear example of RMA's ability to find architecture everywhere and at every scale; it also reflects their method of working. RMA advocates process-oriented design, looks for innovation in process, and sees its role as a problem solver. These are not new ambitions for architecture. Nor is their interest in circulation as a primary driver of all of their buildings a unique idea. And RMA's willingness to wrestle with rule-bound agencies and to fight for code changes that make for better design is the dirty work—the "someone's gotta do it" attitude—that seldom brings recognition. But it does lead to better projects and better public spaces, and to the kinds of results that get a firm invited to a prestigious national competition.

From the entry sequence at the Studio Museum in Harlem to the open stair in the new Stephen Gaynor School, it is easy to see how RMA's design sensibility moves adroitly from building to streetscape to public space projects. The colorful, multistory Gaynor stairway both facilitates and is absorbed into the daily functioning of the special education school, just as the Wall Street security program, although ever-present, disappears into the hubbub of everyday life. The double pavilions of the Eisenhower proposal may have been judged as having too much presence, but as a still-young firm able to work at the multiple scales of the city, where architecture, and the opportunity for architecture, is everywhere, there is no question that Rogers Marvel Architects have initiated a quietly growing design presence at every scale.

Jonathan Marvel and Rob Rogers collaboratively lead a multidisciplinary practice of architects, landscape architects, urban designers, preservationists, and product designers dedicated to critical design thinking in the public and private realms. Winner of the prestigious Fossi Fellowship, Rogers graduated with dual B.A./B.Arch. degrees from Rice University in 1983 and received an M.Des. from the Harvard Graduate School of Design in 1989. Marvel received a B.A. degree from Dartmouth College in 1982, and graduated with distinction with an M.Arch degree from the Harvard Graduate School of Design in 1986.

They built their early careers in other practices: Rogers at I. M. Pei & Partners and Marvel at Richard Meier & Partners Architects. Entrepreneurial in spirit, they each opened independent practices, became close friends while working together on national competitions, and joined forces in 1992. Rogers Marvel Architects has received critical acclaim, including the American Institute of Architects New York Chapter's Medal of Honor, "for their steadfast commitment to design excellence on all scales ranging from furniture to building to planning and landscape." Their exploration in industrial design led them to create TRUCK Product Architecture, and in 2004, they received patents under their company Rock 12 Security Architecture.

They have cotaught design studios for over fifteen years at schools such as Pratt, Columbia, Harvard, Rice, Washington University in St. Louis, and Syracuse University and have led a studio at Parsons The New School of Design for the last ten years. They are active in their communities. Marvel serves on the preservation committee of the Municipal Art Society; on the streetscape committee for the New York City Art Commission; on the NYSCA Architecture, Planning and Design panel; and as a peer reviewer at the NYC DDC Design Excellence Program. Rogers, a GSA Peer since 2003, serves on the 21st Century Embassy Task Force and is a fellow of the American Institute of Architects. Together they frequently lecture at universities and institutions.

Associates and Directors
—

Thomas Baker
Thaddeus Briner
Alissa Bucher
Jennifer Carpenter
Eugene Colberg
Scott Demel
Susannah Drake
Guido Hartray
Vincent Lee
John McLeod
Beth O'Neill
Carol Patterson
Matthew Peckham
Bodil Pedersen
Timothy Rowan
Marta Sanders
Chad Smith
Graeme Waitzkin
Aaron Young

Past and Present
—

Ibrahim Akcora
Jena Akin
Dubravka Antic
Marlon Aranda
Kristen Aronsson
Justin Barent
Rachel Barnard
Jordan Barr
Phillipe Baumann
David Black
Daniel Bradley
Elena Brescia
Peter Buchholz
Jennifer Bunsa
Megan Burke
Martha Bush
Eddie Chiu-Fai Can
Kathleen Cella
Camilo Cerro
Sari Chang
Marissa Cheng
Tak Cheung
Arthur Chu
Steven Chua
Johan Chung
Peter Cirincione
William Clement
Kelly Convery
Chris Dameron
Christoph Dewald
Elizabeth Dietz
Joseph DiNapoli
Patricia Ebner
Matias Estrany
Barrett R. Feldman
Kate Fillin-Yeh
Roland Flores
Mary Franzosa
Timothy Fryatt
Jennifer Ganley
Nambi Gardner
Lihi Gerstner
Scott Glass
Nebil Gokcebay
Zack Griffin
Fritz Haeg
Karyssa Halstead
James Hartford
Corey Hoelker
Brian Hogan
Mary Ann Holliday
Timothy Hull

Carey Jackson-Yonce
Mike Jacobs
Tenzin Jangtey
Daekyung Jo
Josh Kaplan
Carolynn Karp
Kip Katich
Makiko Kawaguchi
Stephen Kawalek
Vanessa Keith
Tanya Khokhar
Jung Kim
Stephen Kredell
Marsh Kriplen
Chian-ju Ku
Phoebe Kung
Trevor Laubenstein
Nida Lee
Philip Lee
Elizabeth Lenell Davies
Timo Lindman
Joanna Lo
Gary Machicek
Elsa Marvel
Jennifer Massim
Nicholas McDermott
Elizabeth McDonald
Edward McGrath
Jose Menendez
Tomas Michalski
Megan Mills
Emma Morris
Liat Muller
Amy Nanni
Robert Nelson
Shane Neufeld
Brenda November
Megan Noyes
Mark Nye
Hallory Paul
Ryan Pauly
Susan Perschino
Robert Pietrocola
Michael Pilarski
Erin Porter
Kristin Proeger
Richard Ramsey
Caroline Razook
Allison Reeves
Benjamin Regnier
Jason Ro
Candice Ross

Michael Russo
Gretchen Schneider
Margaret Scholer
Dakota Shepard
Maiko Shimizu
Jacob Sinclair
Eban Singer
Lissa So
Christopher SooHoo
Brien Strelau
Lisa Su
So Sugita
Shuji Suzumori
Annie Tan
Chi-Ho Tang
Lisa Tanno
Steve Tannenbaum
Ashley Thorfinnson
Ray Thorsland
Gary Tran
Minh Tran
Caitlin Travers
Ed Tung
Audra Tuskes
Haily Tweedie
Renee Valdres
Phoebe Ventouras
Edna Vuong
Keiko Vuong
Paul Wang
Elle White
Noel Williams
Rhiannon Willson
Sarah Wilson
Christian Wofford
Jenny Wu

All otherwise uncredited
images are property of Rogers
Marvel Architects

Paul Warchol:
4–5, 6–7, 21, 22–23, 25, 26–27,
28, 30–31, 50, 51, 95, 101, 102–3,
104–5, 130 top and bottom left,
131 top right, 147, 150, 153, 155,
157, 167–68, 169, 170–71

David Sundberg:
2–3, 33, 37, 45, 46–47, 52, 53,
54–55, 82–83, 85, 86, 87, 88–89,
90, 91, 92–93, 107, 108 bottom,
109, 110–11, 112, 113, 115, 117, 118,
119, 120–21, 123, 125, 126, 127,
128–29, 182 bottom left

Nathan Sayers:
38, 39, 41–2, 43, 135, 136–37,
140–41, 142, 143, 144, 145,
158–59

Paul Hester & Lisa Hardaway:
56–57, 59, 61

Albert Vecerka:
62–63, 64–65, 66, 67, 79 bottom
right, 96, 98–99

Stratton Mountain Resort:
70 bottom left

David Joseph:
78 top left

Danny Bright:
79 top right

Courtesy Kate Spade:
130 top right

Reto Halme:
130 bottom right, 131 bottom
right

Richard Sylvarnes:
131 bottom left

Rock Twelve Security
Architecture and The Macton
Corporation:
149 middle row

Rogers Marvel Architects
and West 8:
162 bottom

ESCO; Zodiac Aerospace:
156 top right

Picture Collection © The New
York Public Library; Astor; Lenox
and Tilden Foundations:
page 148 top

dbox, inc.:
183 top right

pp. 2–3: State Street 14 Townhouses
pp. 4–5: Metropolitan Tower
pp. 6–7: Battery Park City Streetspace

Published by
Princeton Architectural Press
37 East 7th Street
New York, NY 10003

For a free catalog of books, call 1-800-722-6657
Visit our website at www.papress.com

© 2011 Princeton Architectural Press
All rights reserved
Printed and bound in China
14 13 12 11   4 3 2 1   First edition

Editor: Dan Simon
Designer: Paul Wagner

Special thanks to: Bree Anne Apperley,
Sara Bader, Nicola Bednarek Brower,
Janet Behning, Megan Carey, Carina Cha,
Tom Cho, Penny (Yuen Pik) Chu, Russell Fernandez,
Jan Haux, Linda Lee, John Myers, Katharine Myers,
Margaret Rogalski, Andrew Stepanian,
Jennifer Thompson, Joseph Weston, and
Deb Wood of Princeton Architectural Press
—Kevin C. Lippert, publisher

Library of Congress Cataloging-in-Publication Data
Rogers, Rob, 1959–
Rogers Marvel Architects / Rob Rogers and Jonathan
Marvel. — 1st ed.
    p.   cm.
ISBN 978-1-56898-999-0
1. Rogers Marvel Architects (Firm) 2. Architecture—
United States—History—20th century. 3.
Architecture—United States—History—21st century.
I. Marvel, Jonathan. II. Title.
NA737.R593A4 2011
720.92′2—dc22

                    2010034349